3-17-2001

Dear Kathy,

For my dear sister in Christ

In His love and service,

Carole Hayes

Saviour

Saviour

The Life of Christ in Words
and Paintings

Compiled by Philip Law

LOYOLAPRESS.
CHICAGO

Text copyright © 2000. Text by Philip Law. Original edition published under the title *Saviour* by Lion Publishing plc, Oxford, England.

Copyright © Lion Publishing plc 2000.

First published in North America by
LOYOLAPRESS.
3441 N. Ashland Ave., Chicago, IL 60657
ISBN 0-8294-1561-0

First edition 2000
10 9 8 7 6 5 4 3 2 1 0

Typeset in 8.5/12 Calligraphic 810
Printed and bound in Singapore

Acknowledgments
    Extracts from the Authorized Version of the Bible
(The King James Bible), the rights in which are vested in
the Crown, are reproduced by permission of the Crown's
Patentee, Cambridge University Press.
    'Alone to sacrifice thou goest, Lord...' by Peter Abelard,
from *Medieval Latin Lyrics* by Helen Waddell, translator.
Copyright © 1929 by Helen Waddell. Reprinted by
permission of W.W. Norton and Company, Inc. and
Constable Publishers: page 80
    'Pilate' by Mervyn Morris, reproduced by permission
of Dangaroo Press: page 68.

    © The National Gallery, London, England: Cover, pages
3, 5 (detail), 7, 9, 10–11, 15, 27, 31, 33, 35, 39, 41, 42–43, 47,
51 (detail), 53, 55, 65, 67, 71, 73, 81, 83, 85, 87, 90–91, 95, 96.
    SuperStock: pages 13 (Palatina Gallery, Florence, Italy),
17 (Galleria degli Uffizi, Florence, Italy), 18–19 (detail)
(Musée des Beaux-Arts, Dijon, France), 21 (Museo di San
Marco, Florence, Italy), 22–23 (Galleria degli Uffizi,
Florence, Italy), 25 (Musée Ingres, Montauban, France),
29 (Barnes Foundation, Merion, Pennsylvania, USA),
37 (National Gallery of Art, Washington, D.C., USA),
45 (Capodimonte Gallery, Naples, Italy/Mauro Magliani),
49 (National Gallery of Scotland, Edinburgh, Scotland),
57 (Frederiksborgmuseum, Denmark), 59 (Musée du
Louvre, Paris, France), 61 (Arena Chapel, Cappella degli
Scrovegni, Padua, Italy), 63 (Royal Chapel, Granada, Spain),
69 (Scuola Grande di San Rocco, Venice, Italy), 75 (Pitti
Palace, Florence, Italy), 77 (Musée du Louvre, Paris, France),
79 (Pinacoteca di Brera, Milan, Italy/Mauro Magliani),
88–89 (Udine Art Gallery, Italy), 93 (Museo de Art, Ponce,
Puerto Rico).

Contents

LIGHT OF THE WORLD

In the beginning was the Word, and the Word was with God, and the Word was God. The same was in the beginning with God. All things were made by him; and without him was not any thing made that was made. In him was life; and the life was the light of men. And the light shineth in darkness; and the darkness comprehended it not...

He came unto his own, and his own received him not. But as many as received him, to them gave he power to become the sons of God, even to them that believe on his name: which were born, not of blood, nor of the will of the flesh, nor of the will of man, but of God. And the Word was made flesh, and dwelt among us, (and we beheld his glory, the glory as of the only begotten of the Father,) full of grace and truth.

John 1:1–5, 11–14

Paris Bordone (c. 1500–71),
Christ as the Light of the World

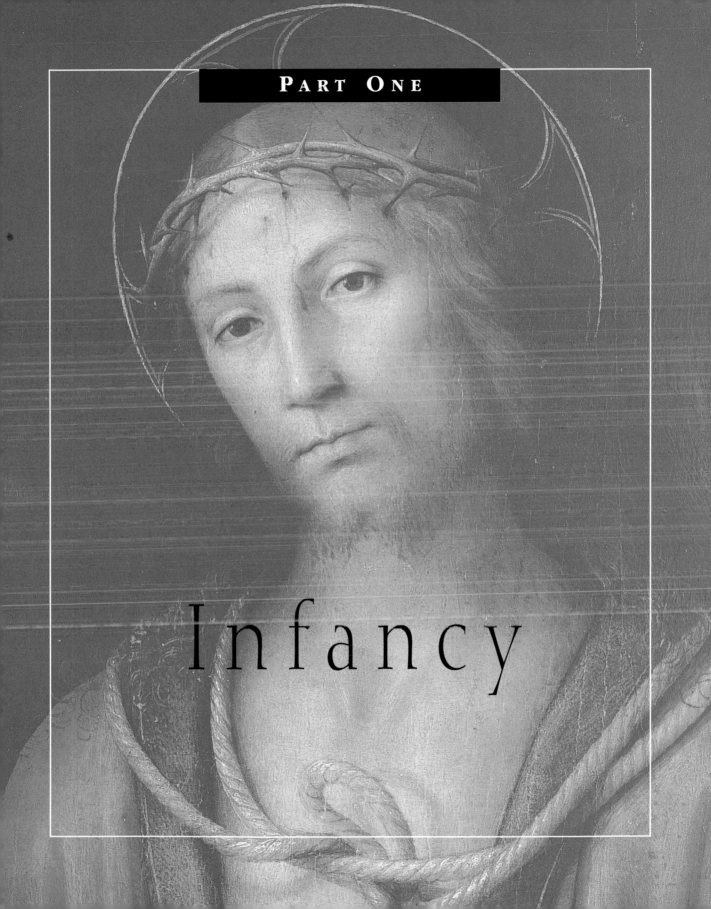

PART ONE

Infancy

ANNUNCIATION

The angel Gabriel was sent from God unto a city of Galilee, named Nazareth, to a virgin espoused to a man whose name was Joseph, of the house of David; and the virgin's name was Mary. And the angel came in unto her, and said, Hail, thou that art highly favoured, the Lord is with thee: blessed art thou among women.

And when she saw him, she was troubled at his saying, and cast in her mind what manner of salutation this should be. And the angel said unto her, Fear not, Mary: for thou hast found favour with God. And, behold, thou shalt conceive in thy womb, and bring forth a son, and shalt call his name Jesus. He shall be great, and shall be called the Son of the Highest: and the Lord God shall give unto him

the throne of his father David: and he shall reign over the house of Jacob for ever; and of his kingdom there shall be no end.

Then said Mary unto the angel, How shall this be, seeing I know not a man?

And the angel answered and said unto her, The Holy Ghost shall come upon thee, and the power of the Highest shall

overshadow thee: therefore also that holy thing
which shall be born of thee shall be called the Son
of God...

And Mary said, Behold the handmaid of the
Lord; be it unto me according to thy word. And
the angel departed from her.

Luke 1:26–35, 38

Today is revealed the mystery that is from all eternity.
The Son of God becomes the Son of Man;
Sharing in what is lower,
He makes me share in what is higher.
Once Adam was deceived:
He sought to become God, but failed.
Now God becomes man,
So as to make Adam God.
Let creation rejoice and nature exult:
For the Archangel stands in fear before the Virgin,
And with his salutation 'Hail!' he brings
The joyful greeting whereby our sorrow is healed.
O God, made man in merciful compassion:
Glory to thee!

From Orthodox Matins for the Feast

MADONNA AND CHILD

And it came to pass in those days, that there went out a decree from Caesar Augustus, that all the world should be taxed. (And this taxing was first made when Cyrenius was governor of Syria.) And all went to be taxed, every one into his own city.

And Joseph also went up from Galilee, out of the city of Nazareth, into Judea, unto the city of David, which is called Bethlehem; (because he was of the house and lineage of David:) to be taxed with Mary his espoused wife, being great with child.

And so it was, that, while they were there, the days were accomplished that she should be delivered.

And she brought forth her firstborn son, and wrapped him in swaddling clothes, and laid him in a manger; because there was no room for them in the inn.

Luke 2:1–7

Comfort is here; help has come down from heaven. 'The kindness and humanity of God our Saviour hath appeared.'

The kindness was always there, for the Lord's mercy is from everlasting; but it was hidden till the humanity appeared. Before that, it was promised, but it was not felt; and many for that reason disbelieved in it. But lo, peace is no longer promised now, but sent; it is no longer prophesied, it is presented to us. God the Father has sent to earth a sackful of his mercy, as it were; a sack that in the passion must be rent, so that the price of our redemption may pour out of it. Only a little sack it is, but it is full. To us a child is given indeed, but in him dwells the fullness of the Godhead. For when the fullness of the time was come, the fullness of the Godhead came also. He came in flesh, to show himself to people living in the flesh; and his humanity appeared that we might know his kindness. For how could he commend his kindness to me better than by taking my flesh – my flesh, not such as Adam had before he fell? What could so mightily declare his mercy as this assumption of our misery? And the smaller he made himself, so much the kinder did he show himself; the smaller, too, that he is made for me, so much the dearer is he.

Bernard of Clairvaux (1090–1153)

Raphael (c. 1483–1520),
Madonna del Granduca

ADORATION OF
THE SHEPHERDS

And there were in the same country shepherds abiding in the field, keeping watch over their flock by night. And, lo, the angel of the Lord came upon them, and the glory of the Lord shone round about them: and they were sore afraid.

And the angel said unto them, Fear not: for, behold, I bring you good tidings of great joy, which shall be to all people. For unto you is born this day in the city of David a Saviour, which is Christ the Lord. And this shall be a sign unto you; ye shall find the babe wrapped in swaddling clothes, lying in a manger. And suddenly there was with the angel a multitude of the heavenly host praising God, and saying, Glory to God in the highest, and on earth peace, good will toward men.

And it came to pass, as the angels were gone away from them into heaven, the shepherds said one to another, Let us now go even unto Bethlehem, and see this thing which is come to pass, which the Lord hath made known unto us. And they came with haste, and found Mary, and Joseph, and the babe lying in a manger.

And when they had seen it, they made known abroad the saying which was told them concerning this child. And all they that heard it wondered at those things which were told them by the shepherds.

But Mary kept all these things, and pondered them in her heart. And the shepherds returned, glorifying and praising God for all the things that they had heard and seen, as it was told unto them.

Luke 2:8–20

AT BETHLEHEM

Come, we shepherds, whose blest sight
*   Hath met Love's noon in nature's night;*
Come, lift we up our loftier song,
And wake the sun that lies too long.

Gloomy night embraced the place
*   Where the noble Infant lay:*
The Babe looked up and showed his face;
*   In spite of darkness, it was day:–*
It was thy Day, Sweet! and did rise
Not from the east, but from thine eyes.

We saw thee in thy balmy nest,
*   Young dawn of our eternal day;*
We saw thine eyes break from their east,
*   And chase the trembling shades away;*
*   We saw thee, (and we bless the sight),*
We saw thee by thine own sweet light.

Welcome, all wonders in one sight!
*   Eternity shut in a span!*
Summer in winter! Day in night!
Heaven in earth! and God in man!
Great Little One, whose all-embracing birth,
Lifts earth to heaven, stoops heaven to earth.

*   Richard Crashaw (1613–50)*

Italian (Neapolitan),
The Adoration of the Shepherds, c. 1630

14

ADORATION OF THE KINGS

Now when Jesus was born in Bethlehem of Judea in the days of Herod the king, behold, there came wise men from the east to Jerusalem, saying, Where is he that is born King of the Jews? for we have seen his star in the east, and are come to worship him.

When Herod the king had heard these things, he was troubled, and all Jerusalem with him. And when he had gathered all the chief priests and scribes of the people together, he demanded of them where Christ should be born. And they said unto him, In Bethlehem of Judea: for thus it is written by the prophet, And thou Bethlehem, in the land of Juda, art not the least among the princes of Juda: for out of thee shall come a Governor, that shall rule my people Israel.

Then Herod, when he had privily called the wise men, enquired of them diligently what time the star appeared. And he sent them to Bethlehem, and said, Go and search diligently for the young child; and when ye have found him, bring me word again, that I may come and worship him also.

When they had heard the king, they departed; and, lo, the star, which they saw in the east, went before them, till it came and stood over where the young child was.

When they saw the star, they rejoiced with exceeding great joy. And when they were come into the house, they saw the young child with Mary his mother, and fell down, and worshipped him: and when they had opened their treasures, they presented unto him gifts; gold, and frankincense, and myrrh. And being warned of God in a dream that they should not return to Herod, they departed into their own country another way.

Matthew 2:1–12

ROYAL PRESENTS

The off'rings of the Eastern kings of old
Unto our lord were incense, myrrh and gold;
Incense because a God; gold as a king;
And myrrh as to a dying man they bring.
Instead of incense (blessed Lord) if we
Can send a sigh or fervent prayer to thee,
Instead of myrrh if we can but provide
Tears that from penitential eyes do slide,
And though we have no gold; if for our part
We can present thee with a broken heart
Thou wilt accept: and say those Eastern kings
Did not present thee with more precious things.

Nathaniel Wanley (1634–80)

Albrecht Dürer (1471–1528),
The Adoration of the Magi

PRESENTATION IN THE TEMPLE

And when eight days were accomplished for the circumcizing of the child, his name was called Jesus, which was so named of the angel before he was conceived in the womb. And when the days of her purification according to the law of Moses were accomplished, they brought him to Jerusalem, to present him to the Lord; (as it is written in the law of the Lord, Every male that openeth the womb shall be called holy to the Lord;) and to offer a sacrifice according to that which is said in the law of the Lord, A pair of turtledoves, or two young pigeons.

And, behold, there was a man in Jerusalem, whose name was Simeon; and the same man was just and devout, waiting for the consolation of Israel: and the Holy Ghost was upon him. And it was revealed unto him by the Holy Ghost, that he should not see death, before he had seen the Lord's Christ.

And he came by the Spirit into the temple: and when the parents brought in the child Jesus, to do for him after the custom of the law, then took he him up in his arms, and blessed God, and said, Lord, now lettest thou thy servant depart in peace, according to thy word: For mine eyes have seen thy salvation, which thou hast prepared before the face of all people; a light to lighten the Gentiles, and the glory of thy people Israel.

Luke 2:21–32

Melchior Broederlam
(active 1381; d. 1409),
Presentation at the Temple
(detail of triptych)

THE PRESENTATION
IN THE TEMPLE

Simeon the just and the devout,
    Who frequent in the fane
Had for the Saviour waited long,
    But waited still in vain.

Came Heaven-directed at the hour
    When Mary held her Son,
He stretched forth his aged arms,
    While tears of gladness run:

With holy joy upon his face
    The good old father smiled,
While fondly in his withered arms
    He clasped the promised Child.

'At last my arms embrace my Lord;
    Now let their vigour cease;
At last my eyes my Saviour see,
    Now let them close in peace;

'The Star and Glory of the land
    Hath now begun to shine;
The morning that shall gild the globe
    Breaks on these eyes of mine!'

    Michael Bruce (1746–67)

FLIGHT INTO EGYPT

The angel of the Lord appeareth to Joseph in a dream, saying, Arise, and take the young child and his mother, and flee into Egypt, and be thou there until I bring thee word: for Herod will seek the young child to destroy him.

When he arose, he took the young child and his mother by night, and departed into Egypt: and was there until the death of Herod: that it might be fulfilled which was spoken of the Lord by the prophet, saying, Out of Egypt have I called my son.

Then Herod, when he saw that he was mocked of the wise men, was exceeding wroth, and sent forth, and slew all the children that were in Bethlehem, and in all the coasts thereof, from two years old and under, according to the time which he had diligently enquired of the wise men. Then was fulfilled that which was spoken by Jeremy the prophet, saying, In Rama was there a voice heard, lamentation, and weeping, and great mourning, Rachel weeping for her children, and would not be comforted, because they are not.

Matthew 2:13–18

This execution was sad, cruel and universal: no abatements made for the dire shriekings of the mothers, no tender-hearted soldier was employed, no hard-hearted person was softened by the weeping eyes, and pity-begging looks of those mothers, that wondered how it was possible any person should hurt their pretty sucklings; no connivances there, no protections, or friendships, or consideration, or indulgences, but Herod caused that his own child which was at nurse in the coasts of Bethlehem should bleed to death; which made Augustus Caesar to say, that in Herod's house it were better to be a hog than a child, because the custom of the nation did secure a hog from Herod's knife, but no religion could secure his child.

Jesus, when himself was safe, could also have secured the poor babes of Bethlehem, but yet it did not so please God. He is Lord of his creatures, and hath absolute dominion over our lives, and he had an end of glory to serve upon these babes, and an end of justice upon Herod; and to the children he made such compensation, that they had no reason to complain that they were so soon made stars, when they shined in their little orbs and participations of eternity, for so the sense of the Church hath been that they having died the death of martyrs, though incapable of making the choice, God supplied the defects of their will, by his own entertainment of the thing; that as the misery and their death, so also their glorification might have the same author in the same manner of causality; even by a peremptory and unconditioned determination in these particulars.

Jeremy Taylor (1613–67)

ELONGAVI FVGIENS 7 MANSI INSOLITVDINE . P̃S . XXXXXV . C

SVRGE ACCIPE PVERVM 7 MATREM EI̅ 7 FVGE INEGIPTVM . MACEI . II . C .

HOLY FAMILY

But when Herod was dead, behold, an angel of the Lord appeareth in a dream to Joseph in Egypt, saying, Arise, and take the young child and his mother, and go into the land of Israel: for they are dead which sought the young child's life.

And he arose, and took the young child and his mother, and came into the land of Israel. But when he heard that Archelaus did reign in Judea in the room of his father Herod, he was afraid to go thither: notwithstanding, being warned of God in a dream, he turned aside into the parts of Galilee: and he came and dwelt in a city called Nazareth: that it might be fulfilled which was spoken by the prophets, He shall be called a Nazarene.

Matthew 2:19–23

What were the actual circumstances of his coming? His Mother is a poor woman; she comes to Bethlehem to be taxed, travelling, when her choice would have been to remain at home. She finds there is no room in the inn; she is obliged to betake herself to a stable; she brings forth her firstborn Son, and lays him in a manger. That little babe, so born, so placed, is none other than the Creator of heaven and earth, the Eternal Son of God.

Well, he was born of a poor woman, laid in a manger, brought up to a lowly trade, that of a carpenter; and when he began to preach the Gospel, he had not a place to lay his head; lastly, he was put to death, to an infamous and odious death, the death which criminals then suffered.

For the three last years of his life, he preached, I say, the gospel, as we read in scripture; but he did not begin to do so till he was thirty years old. For the first thirty years of his life, he seems to have lived, just as a poor man would live now. Day after day, season after season, winter and summer, one year and then another, passed on as might happen to any of us. He passed from being a babe

Michelangelo Buonarroti
(1475–1564),
The Holy Family

in arms to being a child, and then he
became a boy, and so he grew up
'like a tender plant', increasing in
wisdom and stature; and then
he seems to have followed the
trade of Joseph his reputed
father; going on in an
ordinary way without
any great occurrence, till
he was thirty years old.
How very wonderful is
all this! that he should
live here, doing nothing
great, so long; living
here, as if for the
sake of living; not
preaching, or collecting
disciples, or apparently
in any way furthering
the cause which
brought him down
from heaven. Doubtless
there were deep and
wise reasons in God's
counsels for his going
on so long in obscurity;
I only mean, that we do
not know them.

John Henry Newman (1801–90)

DISPUTING WITH THE DOCTORS OF THE LAW

Aⁿd the child grew, and waxed strong in spirit, filled with wisdom: and the grace of God was upon him.

Now his parents went to Jerusalem every year at the feast of the passover. And when he was twelve years old, they went up to Jerusalem after the custom of the feast. And when they had fulfilled the days, as they returned, the child Jesus tarried behind in Jerusalem; and Joseph and his mother knew not of it. But they, supposing him to have been in the company, went a day's journey; and they sought him among their kinsfolk and acquaintance.

And when they found him not, they turned back again to Jerusalem, seeking him. And it came to pass, that after three days they found him in the temple, sitting in the midst of the doctors, both hearing them, and asking them questions. And all that heard him were astonished at his understanding and answers. And when they saw him, they were amazed: and his mother said unto him, Son, why hast thou thus dealt with us? behold, thy father and I have sought thee sorrowing.

And he said unto them, How is it that ye sought me? wist ye not that I must be about my Father's business? And they understood not the saying which he spake unto them.

And he went down with them, and came to Nazareth, and was subject unto them: but his mother kept all these sayings in her heart. And Jesus increased in wisdom and stature, and in favour with God and man.

Luke 2:40–52

JESUS IN THE TEMPLE

With his kind mother, who partakes thy woe,
Joseph, turn back; see where your Child doth sit,
Blowing, yea blowing out those sparks of wit
Which himself on the doctors did I bestow.
The Word but lately could not speak, and lo!
It suddenly speaks wonders; whence comes it
That all which was, and all which should be writ,
A shallow-seeming child should deeply know?
His Godhead was not soul to his manhood,
Nor had time mellow'd him to this ripeness;
But as for one which hath a long task, 'tis good,
With the sun to begin his business,
He in his age's morning thus began,
By miracles exceeding power of man.

    John Donne (1571/2–1631)

Jean Auguste Dominique Ingres
(1780–1867),
Jesus Among Doctors (after work by Raphael)

PART TWO

Ministry

BAPTISM

The beginning of the gospel of Jesus Christ, the Son of God; as it is written in the prophets, Behold, I send my messenger before thy face, which shall prepare thy way before thee. The voice of one crying in the wilderness, Prepare ye the way of the Lord, make his paths straight.

John did baptize in the wilderness, and preach the baptism of repentance for the remission of sins. And there went out unto him all the land of Judea, and they of Jerusalem, and were all baptized of him in the river of Jordan, confessing their sins. And John was clothed with camel's hair, and with a girdle of a skin about his loins; and he did eat locusts and wild honey; and preached, saying, There cometh one mightier than I after me, the latchet of whose shoes I am not worthy to stoop down and unloose. I indeed have baptized you with water: but he shall baptize you with the Holy Ghost.

And it came to pass in those days, that Jesus came from Nazareth of Galilee, and was baptized of John in Jordan. And straightway coming up out of the water, he saw the heavens opened, and the Spirit like a dove descending upon him: and there came a voice from heaven, saying, Thou art my beloved Son, in whom I am well pleased. And immediately the Spirit driveth him into the wilderness.

And he was there in the wilderness forty days, tempted of Satan; and was with the wild beasts; and the angels ministered unto him.

Mark 1:1–13

See the hosts of heaven hushed and still, as the all-holy Bridegroom goes down into the Jordan. No sooner is he baptized than he comes up from the waters, his splendour shining forth over the earth. The gates of heaven are opened, and the Father's voice is heard: 'This is my beloved Son in whom I am well pleased.' All who are present stand in awe as they watch the Spirit descend to bear witness to him. O come, all you peoples, worship him. Praise to you, Lord, for your glorious epiphany which brings joy to us all. The whole world has become radiant with the light of your manifestation.

Ephrem the Syrian (c. 306–73)

Paolo Caliari Veronese (c. 1528–88),
Baptism of Christ

TEACHING FROM SIMON PETER'S BOAT

And it came to pass, that, as the people pressed upon him to hear the word of God, he stood by the lake of Gennesaret, and saw two ships standing by the lake: but the fishermen were gone out of them, and were washing their nets.

And he entered into one of the ships, which was Simon's, and prayed him that he would thrust out a little from the land. And he sat down, and taught the people out of the ship.

Luke 5:1–3

And he told his disciples this story: he said, 'There was once a servant who owed his master a great deal of money, and could not pay it, at which the master, being very angry, was going to have this servant sold for a slave. But the servant kneeling down and begging his master's pardon with great sorrow, the master forgave him. Now this same servant had a fellow-servant who owed him a hundred pence, and instead of being kind and forgiving to this poor man, as his master had been to him, he put him in prison for the debt. His master, hearing of it, went to him, and said, "O wicked servant, I forgave you. Why did you not forgive your fellow-servant?" And because he had not done so, his master turned him away with great misery. So,' said our Saviour, 'how can you expect God to forgive you, if you do not forgive others?' This is the meaning of that part of the Lord's Prayer, where we say 'Forgive us our trespasses' – that word means faults – 'as we forgive them that trespass against us.'

And he told them another story, and said: 'There was a certain farmer once, who had a yard, and he went out early in the morning, and agreed with some labourers to work there, all day, for a penny. And bye and bye, when it was later, he went out again and engaged some more labourers on the same terms; and bye and bye went out again; and so on, several times, until the afternoon. When the day was over, and they all came to be paid, those who had worked since morning complained that those who had not begun to work until late in the day had the same money as themselves, and they said it was not fair. But the master said, "Friend, I agreed with you for a penny; and is it less money to you, because I give the same money to another man?"' Our Saviour meant to teach them by this, that people who have done good all their lives long will go to Heaven after they are dead. But that people who have been wicked, because of their being miserable, or not having parents and friends to take care of them when young, and who are truly sorry for it, however late in their lives and pray God to forgive them, will be forgiven and will go to Heaven too. He taught his disciples in these stories, because he knew the people liked to hear them, and would remember what he said better, if he said it in that way.

Charles Dickens (1812–70)

Herman Saftleven (1609–85),
Christ Teaching from St Peter's Boat on the Lake of Gennesaret

THE MIRACULOUS CATCH OF FISH

Now when he had left speaking, he said unto Simon, Launch out into the deep, and let down your nets for a draught. And Simon answering said unto him, Master, we have toiled all the night, and have taken nothing: nevertheless at thy word I will let down the net.

And when they had this done, they inclosed a great multitude of fishes: and their net brake. And they beckoned unto their partners, which were in the other ship, that they should come and help them. And they came, and filled both the ships, so that they began to sink.

When Simon Peter saw it, he fell down at Jesus' knees, saying, Depart from me; for I am a sinful man, O Lord. For he was astonished, and all that were with him, at the draught of the fishes which they had taken: and so was also James, and John, the sons of Zebedee, which were partners with Simon. And Jesus said unto Simon, Fear not; from henceforth thou shalt catch men.

And when they had brought their ships to land, they forsook all, and followed him.

Luke 5:4–11

Christ urges us to mould our lives and our characters in the image of his, if we wish the light of truth to shine in our hearts. So above all else, we should devote ourselves to meditating on the life of Jesus Christ.

The teaching of Christ is better than all the teaching of holy and wise people; and anyone guided by the Spirit will find hidden nourishment there. Many people hear the gospel frequently and yet feel little desire to imitate Christ. This is because they do not possess the Spirit of Christ. Those who wish to understand and savour the words of Christ to the full must ensure that their whole lives conform to the pattern of Christ's life.

People may discuss the doctrine of the Trinity with great theological skill; but if they lack humility, they will displease God. Intellectual arguments do not make people holy and righteous; God wants us to lead good lives. I would rather feel repentance in my heart, than define it with my mind. You could know the entire Bible word for word, and be familiar with every exposition written by scholars; but if you lack the grace and love of God, the knowledge is useless.

We live in a world of shadows. The only reality consists in loving God and serving him alone. The highest wisdom is to seek the kingdom of heaven, rejecting the things of this world. If you pursue riches, and believe they will make you happy, you are pursuing an empty fantasy. It is equally foolish to seek social status and honour, to become a slave to your natural appetites, to prefer a long life over a good life – to set your heart on anything in the world, which will soon pass away. Instead look only towards that place where lasting joy is to be found.

Thomas à Kempis (1380–1471)

Peter Paul Rubens (1577–1640),
The Miraculous Draught of Fishes

THE GOOD SAMARITAN

And, behold, a certain lawyer stood up, and tempted him, saying, Master, what shall I do to inherit eternal life? He said unto him, What is written in the law? how readest thou?

And he answering said, Thou shalt love the Lord thy God with all thy heart, and with all thy soul, and with all thy strength, and with all thy mind; and thy neighbour as thyself. And he said unto him, Thou hast answered right: this do, and thou shalt live. But he, willing to justify himself, said unto Jesus, And who is my neighbour?

And Jesus answering said, A certain man went down from Jerusalem to Jericho, and fell among thieves, which stripped him of his raiment, and wounded him, and departed, leaving him half dead. And by chance there came down a certain priest that way: and when he saw him, he passed by on the other side. And likewise a Levite, when he was at the place, came and looked on him, and passed by on the other side.

But a certain Samaritan, as he journeyed, came where he was: and when he saw him, he had compassion on him, and went to him, and bound up his wounds, pouring in oil and wine, and set him on his own beast, and brought him to an inn, and took care of him.

And on the morrow when he departed, he took out two pence, and gave them to the host, and said unto him, Take care of him; and whatsoever thou spendest more, when I come again, I will repay thee.

Which now of these three, thinkest thou, was neighbour unto him that fell among the thieves?

And he said, He that shewed mercy on him. Then said Jesus unto him, Go, and do thou likewise.

Luke 10:25–37

We cannot know whether or not we love God, although there are strong indications for recognizing that we do love him; but we can know whether we love our neighbour. And be certain that the more advanced you see you are in love for your neighbour the more advanced you will be in the love of God, for the love his Majesty has for us is so great that to repay us for our love of neighbour he will in a thousand ways increase the love we have for him. I cannot doubt this.

It's important for us to walk with careful attention to how we are proceeding in this matter, for if we practise love of neighbour with great perfection, we will have done everything.

Teresa of Avila (1515–82)

Jacopo Bassano
(active c. 1535; d. 1592),
The Good Samaritan

THE PRODIGAL SON

A certain man had two sons: and the younger of them said to his father, Father, give me the portion of goods that falleth to me. And he divided unto them his living. And not many days after the younger son gathered all together, and took his journey into a far country, and there wasted his substance with riotous living.

And when he had spent all, there arose a mighty famine in that land; and he began to be in want. And he went and joined himself to a citizen of that country; and he sent him into his fields to feed swine. And he would fain have filled his belly with the husks that the swine did eat: and no man gave unto him. And when he came to himself, he said, How many hired servants of my father's have bread enough and to spare, and I perish with hunger! I will arise and go to my father, and will say unto him, Father, I have sinned against heaven, and before thee, and am no more worthy to be called thy son: make me as one of thy hired servants.

And he arose, and came to his father. But when he was yet a great way off, his father saw him, and had compassion, and ran, and fell on his neck, and kissed him. And the son said unto him, Father, I have sinned against heaven, and in thy sight, and am no more worthy to be called thy son. But the father said to his servants, Bring forth the best robe, and put it on him; and put a ring on his hand, and shoes on his feet: and bring hither the fatted calf, and kill it; and let us eat, and be merry: for this my son was dead, and is alive again; he was lost, and is found. And they began to be merry.

Now his elder son was in the field: and as he came and drew nigh to the house, he heard musick and dancing. And he called one of the servants, and asked what these things meant. And he said unto him, Thy brother is come; and thy father hath killed the fatted calf, because he hath received him safe and sound. And he was angry, and would not go in: therefore came his father out, and intreated him. And he answering said to his father, Lo, these many years do I serve thee, neither transgressed I at any time thy commandment: and yet thou never gavest me a kid, that I might make merry with my friends: but as soon as this thy son was come, which hath devoured thy living with harlots, thou hast killed for him the fatted calf. And he said unto him, Son, thou art ever with me, and all that I have is thine. It was meet that we should make merry, and be glad: for this thy brother was dead, and is alive again; and was lost, and is found.

Luke 15:11–32

When it is a question of a sinner he does not merely stand still, open his arms and say, 'Come hither'; no, he stands there and waits, as the father of the lost son waited, rather he does not stand and wait, he goes forth to seek, as the shepherd sought the lost sheep, as the woman sought the lost coin. He goes – yet no, he has gone, but infinitely farther than any shepherd or any woman, he went, in sooth, the infinitely long way from being God to becoming man, and that way he went in search of sinners.

Søren Kierkegaard (1813–55)

Pierre Puvis de Chavannes (1824–98),
The Prodigal Son

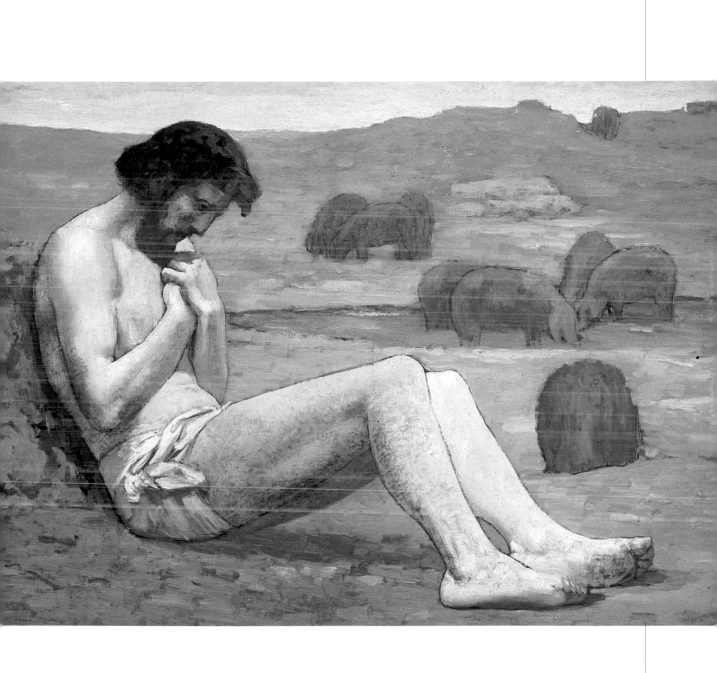

THE PARALYSED MAN

After this there was a feast of the Jews; and Jesus went up to Jerusalem. Now there is at Jerusalem by the sheep market a pool, which is called in the Hebrew tongue Bethesda, having five porches. In these lay a great multitude of impotent folk, of blind, halt, withered, waiting for the moving of the water. For an angel went down at a certain season into the pool, and troubled the water: whosoever then first after the troubling of the water stepped in was made whole of whatsoever disease he had.

And a certain man was there, which had an infirmity thirty and eight years. When Jesus saw him lie, and knew that he had been now a long time in that case, he saith unto him, Wilt thou be made whole? The impotent man answered him, Sir, I have no man, when the water is troubled, to put me into the pool: but while I am coming, another steppeth down before me.

Jesus saith unto him, Rise, take up thy bed, and walk. And immediately the man was made whole, and took up his bed, and walked: and on the same day was the sabbath.

John 5:1–9

The gift of performing miracles takes its key term, 'miracles', from a Greek word meaning 'powers'. A miracle is an event beyond the power of any known physical law to produce; it is a spiritual occurrence produced by the power of God, a marvel, a wonder. In most versions of the Old Testament the word 'miracle' is usually translated 'a wonder' or 'a mighty work'. Versions of the New Testament usually refer to miracles as 'signs' or 'signs and wonders'.

Clearly, the wonders performed by Jesus Christ and the apostles authenticated their claim of authority and gave certitude to their message. And we must remember that people did ask Jesus and the apostles this question, 'How do we know that you are what you say you are, and that your words are true?' That was not an improper question. And at strategic moments God again and again manifested himself to men by miracles so they had outward, confirming evidence that the words they heard from God's servants were true.

Billy Graham (1918–)

Bartolomé Esteban Murillo (1617–82),
Christ Healing the Paralytic at the Pool of Bethesda

THE MAN BORN BLIND

And as Jesus passed by, he saw a man which was blind from his birth. And his disciples asked him, saying, Master, who did sin, this man, or his parents, that he was born blind?

Jesus answered, Neither hath this man sinned, nor his parents: but that the works of God should be made manifest in him. I must work the works of him that sent me, while it is day: the night cometh, when no man can work. As long as I am in the world, I am the light of the world.

When he had thus spoken, he spat on the ground, and made clay of the spittle, and he anointed the eyes of the blind man with the clay, and said unto him, Go, wash in the pool of Siloam, (which is by interpretation, Sent.) He went his way therefore, and washed, and came seeing...

And it was the sabbath day when Jesus made the clay, and opened his eyes. Then again the Pharisees also asked him how he had received his sight. He said unto them, He put clay upon mine eyes, and I washed, and do see.

Therefore said some of the Pharisees, This man is not of God, because he keepeth not the sabbath day. Others said, How can a man that is a sinner do such miracles? And there was a division among them...

And Jesus said, For judgment I am come into this world, that they which see not might see; and that they which see might be made blind. And some of the Pharisees which were with him heard these words, and said unto him, Are we blind also? Jesus said unto them, If ye were blind, ye should have no sin: but now ye say, We see; therefore your sin remaineth.

John 9:1–7, 14–16, 39–41

The thirst of the spirit is chiefly of two kinds, the desire of light and the desire of love. No one surely is without the desire of light. We are all constantly meeting with things which provoke us to ask within ourselves, what is this? how is this? why is this? If we are not curious about such things as books might tell us, we still are troubled with much greater questions. We cannot help seeing what is going on around us among our friends and neighbours, and then we ask how it is that this or that event happens to them. We are still more troubled by thoughts about ourselves and our present and future life. We wonder how a world so full of evil and sorrow can be the work of a good God. This is a longing for light. It is partly satisfied every time that a word spoken by anyone else, or a verse from the Bible, or any other cause gives us a hint which throws light upon what was dark before. And the more we know, the more we desire to know, and then we soon find that there is no teaching like God's own: and all his words and works seem to give forth ever fresh light so long as we remember that they do indeed proceed from him. At last we find that nothing less can satisfy us than God himself to shew us all truth, and we fall on our knees before him, and pray him to scatter all our darkness, and fill us wholly with his own light.

F.J.A. Hort (1828–92)

Duccio di Buoninsegna
(active 1278; d. 1318/19),
Jesus Opens the Eyes of a Man Born Blind

TRIBUTE MONEY

And when they were come to Capernaum, they that received tribute money came to Peter, and said, Doth not your master pay tribute? He saith, Yes. And when he was come into the house, Jesus prevented him, saying, What thinkest thou, Simon? of whom do the kings of the earth take custom or tribute? of their own children, or of strangers? Peter saith unto him, Of strangers.

Jesus saith unto him, Then are the children free. Notwithstanding, lest we should offend them, go thou to the sea, and cast an hook, and take up the fish that first cometh up; and when thou hast opened his mouth, thou shalt find a piece of money: that take, and give unto them for me and thee.

Matthew 17:24–27

This is the gate of righteousness that opens into life, as it is written: 'Open for me the gates of righteousness, that I may go in through them and give praise to the Lord. This is the gate of the Lord: the righteous shall enter it.' So of the many gates through which we may go, that one that is entered through righteousness is the one that is entered through Christ; and happy are all who enter and follow the straight path in holiness and righteousness, doing everything peaceably. Such people should be faithful, should be able to utter truths with real knowledge, should be wise in discernment of what is said, should be pure in deed. For the more highly they are regarded, the more humble a view they should take of themselves, and seek the common good of all, rather than their own advantage.

Clement of Rome (d. c. 95)

Titian (active c. 1506; d. 1576),
The Tribute Money

TITIANVS
F

TRANSFIGURATION

And after six days Jesus taketh with him Peter, and James, and John, and leadeth them up into an high mountain apart by themselves: and he was transfigured before them. And his raiment became shining, exceeding white as snow; so as no fuller on earth can white them. And there appeared unto them Elias with Moses: and they were talking with Jesus.

And Peter answered and said to Jesus, Master, it is good for us to be here: and let us make three tabernacles; one for thee, and one for Moses, and one for Elias. For he wist not what to say; for they were sore afraid. And there was a cloud that overshadowed them: and a voice came out of the cloud, saying, This is my beloved Son: hear him.

And suddenly, when they had looked round about, they saw no man any more, save Jesus only with themselves.

Mark 9:2–8

ACCORDING TO ST MARK

The way was steep and wild; we watched him go
*   Through tangled thicket, over sharp-edged stone*
*   That tore his feet, until he stood alone*
Upon the summit where four great winds blow;
Fearful we knelt on the cold rocks below,
*   For the o'erhanging cloud had larger grown,*
*   A strange still radiance through his body shone*
Whiter than moonlight on the mountain snow.

Then two that flamed amber and amethyst
*   Were either side him, while low thunder rolled*
*   Down to the ravens in their deep ravine;*
But when we looked again, as through a mist
*   We saw him near us. – Like a pearl we hold*
*   Close to our hearts what we have heard and seen.*

Thomas Jones (1882–1932)

Giovanni Bellini (c. 1430–1516),
Transfiguration

THE BLESSING OF THE CHILDREN

And they brought young children to him, that he should touch them: and his disciples rebuked those that brought them.

But when Jesus saw it, he was much displeased, and said unto them, Suffer the little children to come unto me, and forbid them not: for of such is the kingdom of God.

Verily I say unto you, Whosoever shall not receive the kingdom of God as a little child, he shall not enter therein. And he took them up in his arms, put his hands upon them, and blessed them.

Mark 10:13–16

At the same time came the disciples unto Jesus, saying, Who is the greatest in the kingdom of heaven? And Jesus called a little child unto him, and set him in the midst of them, and said, Verily I say unto you, Except ye be converted, and become as little children, ye shall not enter into the kingdom of heaven. Whosoever therefore shall humble himself as this little child, the same is greatest in the kingdom of heaven.

Matthew 18:1–4

When Jesus urged people to repent, he was urging them to become as little children. He wasn't asking them to eat the dust. He was confronting them with the necessity of a radical change of outlook, a fundamental reorientation of their lives, so that they would no longer trust for security in the persona they had built up – the drama of being me which I continuously stage for my own benefit – so that they would no longer trust that, but have the courage to become as receptive as little children, with all the openness to life, the taking down of the shutters and the throwing away of the armour which that entails...

That is what repentance means: discovering that you have more to you than you dreamt or knew, becoming bored with being only a quarter of what you are and therefore taking the risk of surrendering to the whole, and thus finding more abundant life...

It is obvious how important repentance is for the Christian. It was part of the basic message of Jesus. He began his ministry by telling people to repent and believe in the gospel.

Unless, therefore, we are willing to repent, we cannot be his disciples.

H.A. Williams (1919–)

Nicolaes Maes (1634–93),
Christ Blessing the Children

MARTHA AND MARY

Now it came to pass, as they went, that he entered into a certain village: and a certain woman named Martha received him into her house. And she had a sister called Mary, which also sat at Jesus' feet, and heard his word.

But Martha was cumbered about much serving, and came to him, and said, Lord, dost thou not care that my sister hath left me to serve alone? bid her therefore that she help me. And Jesus answered and said unto her, Martha, Martha, thou art careful and troubled about many things: but one thing is needful: and Mary hath chosen that good part, which shall not be taken away from her.

Luke 10:38–42

St Theresa said that to give our Lord a perfect service, Martha and Mary must combine. The modern tendency is to turn from the attitude and the work of Mary; and even call it – as I have heard it called by busy social Christians – a form of spiritual selfishness. Thousands of devoted men and women today believe that the really good part is to keep busy, and give themselves no time to take what is offered to those who abide quietly with Christ; because there seem such a lot of urgent jobs for Martha to do. The result of this can only be a maiming of their human nature, exhaustion, loss of depth and of vision; and it is seen in the vagueness and ineffectuality of a great deal of the work that is done for God. It means a total surrender to the busy click-click of the life of succession; nowhere, in the end, more deadly than in the religious sphere. I insist on this because I feel, more and more, the danger in which we stand of developing a lopsided Christianity; so concentrated on service, and on this-world obligations, as to forget the needs of constant willed and quiet contact with that other world, wherefrom the sanctions of service and the power in which to do it proceed. We mostly spend those lives conjugating three verbs: to Want, to Have, and to Do. Craving, clutching, and fussing, on the material, political, social, emotional, intellectual – even on the religious – plane, we are kept in perpetual unrest: forgetting that none of these verbs has ultimate significance, except so far as they are transcended by and included in, the fundamental verb, to Be: and that Being, not wanting, having, and doing, is the essence of a spiritual life.

Evelyn Underhill (1875–1941)

Jan Vermeer (1632–75),
Christ in the House of Martha and Mary

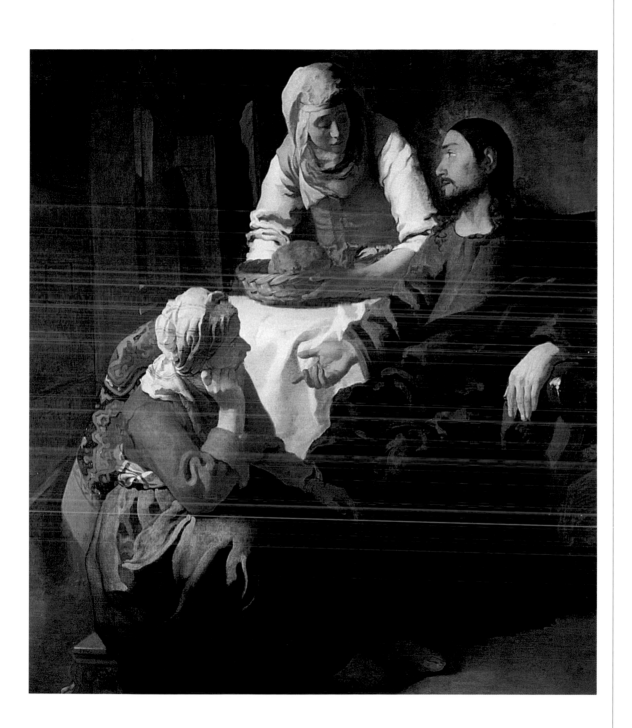

THE ADULTEROUS WOMAN

Jesus went unto the mount of Olives. And early in the morning he came again into the temple, and all the people came unto him; and he sat down, and taught them. And the scribes and Pharisees brought unto him a woman taken in adultery; and when they had set her in the midst, they say unto him, Master, this woman was taken in adultery, in the very act. Now Moses in the law commanded us, that such should be stoned: but what sayest thou? This they said, tempting him, that they might have to accuse him.

But Jesus stooped down, and with his finger wrote on the ground, as though he heard them not. So when they continued asking him, he lifted up himself, and said unto them, He that is without sin among you, let him first cast a stone at her. And again he stooped down, and wrote on the ground.

And they which heard it, being convicted by their own conscience, went out one by one, beginning at the eldest, even unto the last: and Jesus was left alone, and the woman standing in the midst. When Jesus had lifted up himself, and saw none but the woman, he said unto her, Woman, where are those thine accusers? hath no man condemned thee? She said, No man, Lord. And Jesus said unto her, Neither do I condemn thee: go, and sin no more.

John 8:1–11

THE EVERLASTING GOSPEL

Was Jesus Chaste? or did he
Give any Lessons of Chastity?
The morning blush'd fiery red:
Mary was found in Adulterous bed;
Earth groan'd beneath, & Heaven above
Trembled at discovery of Love.

Jesus was sitting in Moses' Chair,
They brought the trembling Woman There.
Moses commands she be stoned to death,
What was the sound of Jesus' breath?
He laid his hand on Moses' Law:
The Ancient Heavens, in Silent Awe
Writ with Curses from Pole to Pole,
All away began to roll:
The Earth trembling & Naked lay
In secret bed of Mortal Clay,
On Sinai felt the hand divine
Putting back the bloody shrine,
And she heard the breath of God
As she heard by Eden's flood:
'Good & Evil are no more!
Sinai's trumpets, cease to roar!
Cease, finger of God, to write!
The Heavens are not clean in thy Sight.
Thou art Good, & Thou Alone;
Nor may the sinner cast one stone.
To be Good only, is to be
A God or else a Pharisee.
Thou Angel of the Presence Divine
That didst create this Body of Mine,
Wherefore hast thou writ these Laws
And Created Hell's dark jaws?
My Presence I will take from thee:
A Cold Leper thou shalt be.
Tho' thou wast so pure & bright
That Heaven was Impure in thy Sight,
Tho' thy Oath turn'd Heaven Pale,
Tho' thy Covenant built Hell's Jail,
Tho' thou didst all to Chaos roll
With the Serpent for its soul,
Still the breath Divine does move
And the breath Divine is Love.'

William Blake (1757–1827)

50

Rembrandt van Rijn (1606–69),
The Woman Taken in Adultery

THE RAISING OF LAZARUS

Now a certain man was sick, named Lazarus, of Bethany, the town of Mary and her sister Martha... When Jesus heard that, he said, This sickness is not unto death, but for the glory of God, that the Son of God might be glorified thereby.

Now Jesus loved Martha, and her sister, and Lazarus. When he had heard therefore that he was sick, he abode two days still in the same place where he was. Then after that saith he to his disciples, Let us go into Judea again... and after that he saith unto them, Our friend Lazarus sleepeth; but I go, that I may awake him out of sleep. Then said his disciples, Lord, if he sleep, he shall do well. Howbeit Jesus spake of his death: but they thought that he had spoken of taking of rest in sleep...

Then when Jesus came, he found that he had lain in the grave four days already. Now Bethany was nigh unto Jerusalem, about fifteen furlongs off: and many of the Jews came to Martha and Mary, to comfort them concerning their brother. Then Martha, as soon as she heard that Jesus was coming, went and met him: but Mary sat still in the house. Then said Martha unto Jesus, Lord, if thou hadst been here, my brother had not died...

When Jesus therefore saw her weeping, and the Jews also weeping which came with her, he groaned in the spirit, and was troubled, and said, Where have ye laid him? They said unto him, Lord, come and see.

Jesus wept. Then said the Jews, Behold how he loved him! And some of them said, Could not this man, which opened the eyes of the blind, have caused that even this man should not have died?

Jesus therefore again groaning in himself cometh to the grave. It was a cave, and a stone lay upon it. Jesus said, Take ye away the stone. Martha, the sister of him that was dead, saith unto him, Lord, by this time he stinketh: for he hath been dead four days...

Then they took away the stone from the place where the dead was laid. And Jesus lifted up his eyes, and said, Father, I thank thee that thou hast heard me. And I knew that thou hearest me always: but because of the people which stand by I said it, that they may believe that thou hast sent me.

And when he thus had spoken, he cried with a loud voice, Lazarus, come forth. And he that was dead came forth, bound hand and foot with graveclothes: and his face was bound about with a napkin. Jesus saith unto them, Loose him, and let him go.

John 11:1, 4–7, 11–13, 17–21, 33–39, 41–44

LAZARUS

When Lazarus left his charnel-cave,
*   And home to Mary's house returned,*
*   Was this demanded – if he yearned*
To hear her weeping by his grave?

'Where wert thou, brother, these four days?'
*   There lives no record of reply,*
*   Which telling what it is to die*
Had surely added praise to praise.

From every house the neighbours met,
*   The streets were filled with joyful sound*
*   A solemn gladness even crowned*
The purple brows of Olivet.

Behold a man raised up by Christ!
*   The rest remaineth unrevealed;*
*   He told it not; or something sealed*
The lips of that Evangelist.

Alfred Tennyson (1809–92)

Sebastiano del Piombo (c. 1485–1547),
The Raising of Lazarus

PART THREE

Passion

CLEANSING THE TEMPLE

And when he was come into Jerusalem, all the city was moved, saying, Who is this? And the multitude said, This is Jesus the prophet of Nazareth of Galilee. And Jesus went into the temple of God, and cast out all them that sold and bought in the temple, and overthrew the tables of the moneychangers, and the seats of them that sold doves, and said unto them, It is written, My house shall be called the house of prayer; but ye have made it a den of thieves.

And the blind and the lame came to him in the temple; and he healed them. And when the chief priests and scribes saw the wonderful things that he did, and the children crying in the temple, and saying, Hosanna to the son of David; they were sore displeased, and said unto him, Hearest thou what these say? And Jesus saith unto them, Yea; have ye never read, Out of the mouth of babes and sucklings thou hast perfected praise? And he left them, and went out of the city into Bethany; and he lodged there.

Matthew 21:10–17

In the action of the cleansing of the Temple the mind of Jesus is clearly revealed to us.

Here Jesus acts as nothing less than the spokesman of God. He did not cleanse the Temple like some church office-bearer or official attacking some abuse or cleaning up some evil and improper situation. He cleansed the Temple *as if it belonged to him*, as if it was his own personal house and dwelling-place. In this action and event Jesus did nothing less than identify his own action with the action of God. He does not act like a man dealing with some abuse; he acts like God sweeping the evil from his own house...

His anger was kindled to a white heat at the sight of simple people cheated, swindled, imposed upon by clever and rapacious scoundrels. Here in this event is the affirmation of the social gospel which regards the exploitation of men as a crime against God.

There is an even deeper condemnation here; there is the condemnation of anything which hinders ordinary people in their search for God.

William Barclay (1907–78)

Carl Heinrich Bloch (1834–90),
Christ Driving the Money Changers Out of the Temple

THE LAST SUPPER

Now the first day of the feast of unleavened bread the disciples came to Jesus, saying unto him, Where wilt thou that we prepare for thee to eat the passover? And he said, Go into the city to such a man, and say unto him, The Master saith, My time is at hand; I will keep the passover at thy house with my disciples.

And the disciples did as Jesus had appointed them; and they made ready the passover.

Now when the even was come, he sat down with the twelve. And as they did eat, he said, Verily I say unto you, that one of you shall betray me. And they were exceeding sorrowful, and began every one of them to say unto him, Lord, is it I? And he answered and said, He that dippeth his hand with me in the dish, the same shall betray me. The Son of man goeth as it is written of him: but woe unto that man by whom the Son of man is betrayed! it had been good for that man if he had not been born. Then Judas, which betrayed him, answered and said, Master, is it I? He said unto him, Thou hast said.

And as they were eating, Jesus took bread, and blessed it, and brake it, and gave it to the disciples, and said, Take, eat; this is my body. And he took the cup, and gave thanks, and gave it to them, saying, Drink ye all of it; for this is my blood of the new testament, which is shed for many for the remission of sins. But I say unto you, I will not drink henceforth of this fruit of the vine, until that day when I drink it new with you in my Father's kingdom.

Matthew 26:17–29

We give you thanks, holy Father,
for your holy name,
which you planted in our hearts;
and for the knowledge, faith and immortality
which you sent us through Jesus Christ, your child.

Glory to you throughout the ages.

You created everything, sovereign Lord,
for the glory of your name.
You gave food and drink to men
for their enjoyment,
and as a cause for thanksgiving.
And to us you have given
spiritual food and spiritual drink,
bestowing on us the promise of eternal life.
Above all we thank you
for the power of your love.

Glory to you throughout the ages.

The Didache (1st or 2nd century)

Frans Pourbus II (1569–1622),
The Last Supper

WASHING THE DISCIPLES' FEET

And supper being ended, the devil having now put into the heart of Judas Iscariot, Simon's son, to betray him; Jesus knowing that the Father had given all things into his hands, and that he was come from God, and went to God; he riseth from supper, and laid aside his garments; and took a towel, and girded himself. After that he poureth water into a bason, and began to wash the disciples' feet, and to wipe them with the towel wherewith he was girded.

Then cometh he to Simon Peter: and Peter saith unto him, Lord, dost thou wash my feet? Jesus answered and said unto him, What I do thou knowest not now; but thou shalt know hereafter. Peter saith unto him, Thou shalt never wash my feet. Jesus answered him, If I wash thee not, thou hast no part with me. Simon Peter saith unto him, Lord, not my feet only, but also my hands and my head. Jesus saith to him, He that is washed needeth not save to wash his feet, but is clean every whit: and ye are clean, but not all. For he knew who should betray him; therefore said he, Ye are not all clean.

So after he had washed their feet, and had taken his garments, and was set down again, he said unto them, Know ye what I have done to you? Ye call me Master and Lord: and ye say well; for so I am. If I then, your Lord and Master, have washed your feet; ye also ought to wash one another's feet. For I have given you an example, that ye should do as I have done to you.

John 13:2–15

It is almost impossible to overestimate the value of true humility and its power in the spiritual life. For the beginning of humility and consummation of humility is the perfection of all joy. Humility contains in itself the answer to all the great problems of the life of the soul. It is the only key to faith, with which the spiritual life begins: for faith and humility are inseparable. In perfect humility all selfishness disappears and your soul no longer lives for itself: and it is lost and submerged in God and transformed into him.

At this point of the spiritual life humility meets the highest exaltation of greatness. It is here that every one who humbles himself is exalted because, living no longer for himself or on the human level, the spirit is delivered of all the limitations and vicissitudes of creaturehood and of contingency, and swims in the attributes of God, whose power, magnificence, greatness and eternity have, through love, through humility, become our own.

Thomas Merton (1915–68)

Giotto di Bondone (1266–1337),
The Washing of the Feet

AGONY IN THE GARDEN

And they came to a place which was named Gethsemane: and he saith to his disciples, Sit ye here, while I shall pray. And he taketh with him Peter and James and John, and began to be sore amazed, and to be very heavy; and saith unto them, My soul is exceeding sorrowful unto death: tarry ye here, and watch. And he went forward a little, and fell on the ground, and prayed that, if it were possible, the hour might pass from him. And he said, Abba, Father, all things are possible unto thee; take away this cup from me: nevertheless not what I will, but what thou wilt.

And he cometh, and findeth them sleeping, and saith unto Peter, Simon, sleepest thou? couldest not thou watch one hour? Watch ye and pray, lest ye enter into temptation. The spirit truly is ready, but the flesh is weak.

And again he went away, and prayed, and spake the same words. And when he returned, he found them asleep again, (for their eyes were heavy,) neither wist they what to answer him.

And he cometh the third time, and saith unto them, Sleep on now, and take your rest: it is enough, the hour is come; behold, the Son of man is betrayed into the hands of sinners. Rise up, let us go; lo, he that betrayeth me is at hand.

Mark 14:32–42

Jesus suffers in his passion the torments which men inflict upon him; but in his agony he suffers the torments which he inflicts on himself; *turbare semetipsum*. This is a suffering from no human, but an almighty hand, for he must be almighty to bear it.

Jesus seeks some comfort at least in his three dearest friends, and they are asleep. He prays them to bear with him for a little, and they leave him with entire indifference, having so little compassion that it could not prevent their sleeping, even for a moment. And thus Jesus was left alone to the wrath of God.

Jesus is alone on the earth, without any one not only to feel and share his suffering, but even to know of it; he and heaven were alone in that knowledge.

Jesus is in a garden, not of delight as the first Adam, where he lost himself and the whole human race, but in one of agony, where he saved himself and the whole human race.

He suffers this affliction and this desertion in the horror of the night.

I believe that Jesus never complained but on this single occasion; but then he complained as if he could no longer bear his extreme suffering. 'My soul is sorrowful, even unto death.'...

Jesus, in the midst of this universal desertion, including that of his own friends chosen to watch with him, finding them asleep, is vexed because of the danger to which they expose, not him, but themselves; he cautions them for their own safety and their own good, with a sincere tenderness for them during their ingratitude, and warns them that the spirit is willing and the flesh weak.

Jesus, finding them still asleep, without being restrained by any consideration for themselves or for him, has the kindness not to waken them, and leaves them in repose.

Jesus prays, uncertain of the will of his Father, and fears death; but when he knows it, he goes forward to offer himself to death.

Blaise Pascal (1623–62)

Sandro Botticelli (c. 1445–1510),
Christ in the Garden of Olives

BETRAYAL AND ARREST

And while he yet spake, lo, Judas, one of the twelve, came, and with him a great multitude with swords and staves, from the chief priests and elders of the people.

Now he that betrayed him gave them a sign, saying, Whomsoever I shall kiss, that same is he: hold him fast.

And forthwith he came to Jesus, and said, Hail, master; and kissed him. And Jesus said unto him, Friend, wherefore art thou come?

Then came they, and laid hands on Jesus and took him. And, behold, one of them which were with Jesus stretched out his hand, and drew his sword, and struck a servant of the high priest's, and smote off his ear. Then said Jesus unto him, Put up again thy sword into his place: for all they that take the sword shall perish with the sword. Thinkest thou that I cannot now pray to my Father, and he shall presently give me more than twelve legions of angels? But how then shall the scriptures be fulfilled, that thus it must be?

In that same hour said Jesus to the multitudes, Are ye come out as against a thief with swords and staves for to take me? I sat daily with you teaching in the temple, and ye laid no hold on me. But all this was done, that the scriptures of the prophets might be fulfilled. Then all the disciples forsook him, and fled. And they that had laid hold on Jesus led him away to Caiaphas the high priest, where the scribes and the elders were assembled.

Matthew 26:47–57

Into the woods my Master went,
Clean forspent, forspent.
Into the woods my Master came,
Forspent with love and shame.
But the olives they were not blind to him,
The little grey leaves were kind to him:
The thorn trees had a mind to him
    When into the woods he came.

Out of the woods my Master went,
And he was well content.
Out of the woods my Master came,
Content with death and shame.
When death and shame would woo him last,
From under the trees they drew him last:
'Twas on a tree they slew him – last
    When out of the woods he came.

  Sidney Lanier (1842–81)

Ugolino di Nerio
(active 1317; d. c. 1339/49),
The Betrayal of Christ

TRIAL BEFORE THE HIGH PRIEST

Now the chief priests, and elders, and all the council, sought false witness against Jesus, to put him to death; but found none: yea, though many false witnesses came, yet found they none.

At the last came two false witnesses, and said, This fellow said, I am able to destroy the temple of God, and to build it in three days. And the high priest arose, and said unto him, Answerest thou nothing? what is it which these witness against thee?

But Jesus held his peace, And the high priest answered and said unto him, I adjure thee by the living God, that thou tell us whether thou be the Christ, the Son of God. Jesus saith unto him, Thou hast said: nevertheless I say unto you, Hereafter shall ye see the Son of man sitting on the right hand of power, and coming in the clouds of heaven.

Then the high priest rent his clothes, saying, He hath spoken blasphemy; what further need have we of witnesses? behold, now ye have heard his blasphemy. What think ye?

They answered and said, He is guilty of death. Then did they spit in his face, and buffeted him; and others smote him with the palms of their hands, saying, Prophesy unto us, thou Christ, Who is he that smote thee?

Matthew 26:59–68

It is with the victim, the condemned, that God identifies, and it is in the company of the victim, so to speak, that God is to be found, and nowhere else. And this is not simply to say, in the fashionable phrase, that God makes his own the cause of the poor and despised. We are not talking of 'the' poor and despised, 'the' victim in the abstract... We are, insistently and relentlessly, in Jerusalem, confronted therefore with a victim who is *our* victim. When we make victims, when we embark on condemnation, exclusion, violence, the diminution or oppression of anyone, when we set ourselves up as judges, we are exposed to judgment (as Jesus himself asserts in Matthew 7:1–2), and we turn away from salvation. To hear the good news of salvation, to be converted, is to turn back to the condemned and rejected, acknowledging that there is hope nowhere else.

Rowan Williams (1950–)

Gerrit van Honthorst (1592–1656),
Christ Before the High Priest

TRIAL BEFORE PILATE

And the whole multitude of them arose, and led him unto Pilate. And they began to accuse him, saying, We found this fellow perverting the nation, and forbidding to give tribute to Caesar, saying that he himself is Christ a King.

And Pilate asked him, saying, Art thou the King of the Jews? And he answered him and said, Thou sayest it.

Then said Pilate to the chief priests and to the people, I find no fault in this man. And they were the more fierce, saying, He stirreth up the people, teaching throughout all Jewry, beginning from Galilee to this place.

Luke 23:1–5

PILATE

And then I tried to pass the buck;
but Herod, with astute aplomb,
politely, sent him back.

I tried to move the people
to accept he might be freed
this feast of 'The Passover'.
'Kill him! Kill him! Nail him
to the cross!' They clamoured for
Barabbas, insurrectionist, a bandit
who's attacked imperial rule.
'Try Jesus for yourselves,' I told the mob;
'You judge him by your law.'

'Kill him,' they hollered louder,
'Nail him to the cross!'
Then slimy priests, those holy rogues
of politics, began to turn the screws:
'You must not fail to sentence Christ,
soi-disant King of Jews.
Your masters wouldn't like it much
if we should let them know
we caught a man supplanting Rome
and you have let him go.'

My basic job is keeping peace
and reverence for Rome. The man
was bad for both. I had to yield.
'I find no fault in him,' I cried,
and ordered water brought;
and, public gesture of defeat
(sound politics, I thought),
I washed these loving
histrionic hands.

The crowd surprised me, seized
the guilt of their demands.

*   You know*
I am not weak. I could, I would
stand up for Jesus if I thought
that were the thing to do. Now
he is dead. He didn't seem to care,
so why should you? How is your head,
my sweet?

Mervyn Morris (1937–)

Jacopo Tintoretto (1518–94),
Christ Before Pilate

THE SUFFERING SERVANT

And Pilate, when he had called together the chief priests and the rulers and the people, said unto them, Ye have brought this man unto me, as one that perverteth the people: and, behold, I, having examined him before you, have found no fault in this man touching those things whereof ye accuse him: no, nor yet Herod: for I sent you to him; and, lo, nothing worthy of death is done unto him. I will therefore chastise him, and release him.

Luke 23:13–16

We can find no greater inspiration to love even our enemies as brothers and sisters – as we must if our love is to be perfect – than grateful remembrance of Christ's wonderful patience. He who was the fairest of the children of men offered his beautiful face to be spat upon by sinners; he allowed those eyes whose glance rules the universe to be blindfolded by wicked men; he bared his back to the scourges; he submitted that head which strikes terror into principalities and powers to the sharpness of thorns; he gave himself up to be mocked and reviled, and at the end endured the cross, the nails, the lance, the gall, the vinegar, while remaining always gentle, kindly, and serene.

In short, he was led like a sheep to the slaughter, and like a lamb before the shearers he was silent, not opening his mouth.

Aelred of Rievaulx (1109–67)

Diego Velázquez (1599–1660),
Christ After the Flagellation
Contemplated by the Christian Soul

71

CROWN OF THORNS

And the soldiers led him away into the hall, called Praetorium; and they call together the whole band. And they clothed him with purple, and platted a crown of thorns, and put it about his head, and began to salute him, Hail, King of the Jews! And they smote him on the head with a reed, and did spit upon him, and bowing their knees worshipped him.

Mark 15:16–19

God is unwearied patience, a meekness that cannot be provoked; he is an ever-enduring mercifulness; he is unmixed goodness, impartial, universal love; his delight is in the communication of himself, his own happiness to everything according to its capacity. He does everything that is good, righteous, and lovely for its own sake, because it is good, righteous and lovely. He is the good from which nothing but good comes, and resisteth all evil only with goodness. This... is the nature and Spirit of God.

William Law (1686–1761)

Attributed to Lo Spagna
(active 1504; d. 1528),
Christ Crowned with Thorns

'BEHOLD THE MAN'

Then came Jesus forth, wearing the crown of thorns, and the purple robe. And Pilate saith unto them, Behold the man! When the chief priests therefore and officers saw him, they cried out, saying, Crucify him, crucify him. Pilate saith unto them, Take ye him, and crucify him: for I find no fault in him. The Jews answered him, We have a law, and by our law he ought to die, because he made himself the Son of God. When Pilate therefore heard that saying, he was the more afraid; and went again into the judgment hall, and saith unto Jesus, Whence art thou? But Jesus gave him no answer.

Then saith Pilate unto him, Speakest thou not unto me? knowest thou not that I have power to crucify thee, and have power to release thee? Jesus answered, Thou couldest have no power at all against me, except it were given thee from above: therefore he that delivered me unto thee hath the greater sin.

And from thenceforth Pilate sought to release him: but the Jews cried out, saying, If thou let this man go, thou art not Caesar's friend: whosoever maketh himself a king speaketh against Caesar. When Pilate therefore heard that saying, he brought Jesus forth, and sat down in the judgment seat in a place that is called the Pavement, but in the Hebrew, Gabbatha.

And it was the preparation of the passover, and about the sixth hour: and he saith unto the Jews, Behold your King! But they cried out, Away with him, away with him, crucify him. Pilate saith unto them, Shall I crucify your King? The chief priests answered, We have no king but Caesar. Then delivered he him therefore unto them to be crucified..And they took Jesus, and led him away.

John 19:5–16

If we look at the gospel story of the Passion as a whole and do not isolate the Cross from its context, one of the most impressive and revealing things in it is the air of strong deliberation and mastery which characterizes Jesus throughout those last days. He is so manifestly not in the least a straw on the stream of events. His enemies are not manipulating him so much as he is manipulating them, not in any wrong way, but in the way in which God does lay hold of the wrath and sin of man and make them subserve his infinite purpose of love. To the end he could have escaped the Cross by the simple expedient of going somewhere else; but he did not do so. He deliberately directs his steps to it. There is an atmosphere of mastery all about him as he steadfastly sets his face towards Jerusalem.

Standing before the council, or before Pilate, there is no suggestion of fumbling or hesitancy. Nor on the other hand is there any suggestion of a merely excited and fanatical confidence. It is the other people who are excited, not he. And it is always the excited people who are the weak people. He says almost regally, 'No man taketh my life from me; I lay it down of myself.' He says – very plainly, quietly, with the direct steadiness of clear-sighted conviction – 'Hereafter ye shall see the Son of man seated at the right hand of power.' The hereafter refers to their seeing. He himself sees now. He is conscious of being in a very real sense at the right hand of power now. He is with God now; the victory is his now.

H.H. Farmer (20th century)

Antonio Ciseri (1821–91),
Ecce Homo

PROCESSION TO CALVARY

As they led him away, they laid hold upon one Simon, a Cyrenian, coming out of the country; and on him they laid the cross, that he might bear it after Jesus.

And there followed him a great company of people, and of women, which also bewailed and lamented him. But Jesus turning unto them said, Daughters of Jerusalem, weep not for me, but weep for yourselves, and for your children. For, behold, the days are coming in which they shall say, Blessed are the barren, and the wombs that never bare... Then shall they begin to say to the mountains, Fall on us; and to the hills, Cover us. For if they do these things in a green tree, what shall be done in the dry?

Luke 23:26–31

Everything in the present moment tends to draw us away from the path of love and passive obedience. It requires heroic courage and self-surrender to hold firmly to a simple faith and to keep singing the same tune confidently while grace itself seems to be singing a different one in another key, giving us the impression that we have been misled and are lost. But if only we have the courage to let the thunder, lightning and storm rage, and to walk unfaltering in the path of love and obedience to the duty and demands of the present moment, we are emulating Jesus himself. For we are sharing that passion during which our Saviour walked with equal firmness and courage in the love of his father and in obedience to his will, submitting to treatment which seemed utterly opposed to the dignity of so holy a saint.

Jesus and Mary, on that dark night, let the storm break over them, a deluge which, in apparent opposition to God's will, harms them. They march undaunted in the path of love and obedience, keeping their eyes on what they have to do, and leaving God to do what he will. They groan under the weight of the divine action, but do not falter or stop for a single moment, believing that all will be well providing they keep on their course and leave the rest to God.

Jean Pierre de Caussaude (1675–1751)

Pierre Mignard I (1612–95),
Christ Bearing the Cross

CRUCIFIXION

And there were also two other, malefactors, led with him to be put to death. And when they were come to the place, which is called Calvary, there they crucified him, and the malefactors, one on the right hand, and the other on the left.

Then said Jesus, Father, forgive them; for they know not what they do. And they parted his raiment, and cast lots. And the people stood beholding. And the rulers also with them derided him, saying, He saved others; let him save himself, if he be Christ, the chosen of God. And the soldiers also mocked him, coming to him, and offering him vinegar, and saying, If thou be the king of the Jews, save thyself. And a superscription also was written over him in letters of Greek, and Latin, and Hebrew, THIS IS THE KING OF THE JEWS...

And it was about the sixth hour, and there was a darkness over all the earth until the ninth hour. And the sun was darkened, and the veil of the temple was rent in the midst. And when Jesus had cried with a loud voice, he said, Father, into thy hands I commend my spirit: and having said thus, he gave up the ghost. Now when the centurion saw what was done, he glorified God, saying, Certainly this was a righteous man. And all the people that came together to that sight, beholding the things which were done, smote their breasts, and returned. And all his acquaintance, and the women that followed him from Galilee, stood afar off, beholding these things.

Luke 23:32–38, 44–49

Awake now, O my soul, shake thyself from the dust, and with deeper attention contemplate this wondrous Man whom, in the glass of the gospel story, thou, as it were, gazest upon, present before thee. Consider, O my soul, who he is, who walketh with the fashion as it were of a king; and nevertheless is filled with the confusion of a most despised slave. He goeth crowned: but his very crown is a torture to him and woundeth with a thousand punctures his most glorious head... See further how in all things he is constrained, spit upon, despised. He is bid to bend his neck beneath the burden of his Cross, and he himself to bear his own ignominy. Brought to the place of punishment, he is given to drink myrrh and gall. He is lifted up upon the Cross and he saith, 'Father, forgive them, they know not what they do.' What manner of man is this, who in all his afflictions never once opened his mouth to utter a word of complaint or pleading, or of threatening or cursing against those accursed dogs, and last of all poured forth over his enemies a word of blessing such as hath not been heard from the beginning? What more gentle than this man, what more kind, O my soul, hast thou seen? Gaze on him, however, yet more intently, for he seemeth worthy both of great admiration and of most tender compassion. See him stripped naked, and torn with stripes, between thieves ignominiously fixed with nails of iron to the Cross, given vinegar to drink upon the Cross, and after death pierced in his side with the spear, and pouring forth plentiful streams of blood from the five wounds of his hands and feet and side. Pour down your tears, mine eyes; melt, O my soul, with the fire of compassion at the sufferings of that Man of love, whom in the midst of such gentleness thou seest afflicted with so bitter griefs.

Anselm of Canterbury (1033–1109)

Bartolommeo Suardi Bramantino
(c. 1465–1530), *Crucifixion*

ENTOMBMENT

And, behold, there was a man named Joseph, a counsellor; and he was a good man, and a just: (The same had not consented to the counsel and deed of them;) he was of Arimathea, a city of the Jews: who also himself waited for the kingdom of God. This man went unto Pilate, and begged the body of Jesus. And he took it down, and wrapped it in linen, and laid it in a sepulchre that was hewn in stone, wherein never man before was laid. And that day was the preparation, and the sabbath drew on. And the women also, which came with him from Galilee, followed after, and beheld the sepulchre, and how his body was laid. And they returned, and prepared spices and ointments; and rested the sabbath day according to the commandment.

Luke 23:50–56

This is that night of tears, the three days' space,
*   Sorrow abiding of the eventide,*
Until the day break with the risen Christ,
*   And hearts that sorrowed shall be satisfied.*

So may our hearts share in thine anguish, Lord,
*   That they may sharers of thy glory be:*
Heavy with weeping may the three days pass,
*   To win the laughter of thine Easter Day.*

Peter Abelard (1079–1142)

Sisto Badalocchio
(1528–after 1621?),
Christ Carried to the Tomb

Glory

RESURRECTION

In the end of the sabbath, as it began to dawn toward the first day of the week, came Mary Magdalene and the other Mary to see the sepulchre. And, behold, there was a great earthquake: for the angel of the Lord descended from heaven, and came and rolled back the stone from the door, and sat upon it. His countenance was like lightning, and his raiment white as snow: and for fear of him the keepers did shake, and became as dead men. And the angel answered and said unto the women, Fear not ye: for I know that ye seek Jesus, which was crucified. He is not here: for he is risen, as he said. Come, see the place where the Lord lay. And go quickly, and tell his disciples that he is risen from the dead; and, behold, he goeth before you into Galilee; there shall ye see him: lo, I have told you. And they departed quickly from the sepulchre with fear and great joy; and did run to bring his disciples word...

Now when they were going, behold, some of the watch came into the city, and shewed unto the chief priests all the things that were done. And when they were assembled with the elders, and had taken counsel, they gave large money unto the soldiers, saying, Say ye, His disciples came by night, and stole him away while we slept. And if this come to the governor's ears, we will persuade him, and secure you. So they took the money, and did as they were taught: and this saying is commonly reported among the Jews until this day.

Matthew 28:1–8, 11–15

AT THE SEPULCHRE

Ye humble souls that seek the Lord,
*   Chase all your fears away;*
And bow with pleasure down to see
*   The place where Jesus lay.*

Thus low the Lord of life was brought;
*   Such wonders Love can do;*
Thus cold in death that bosom lay,
*   Which throbb'd and bled for you.*

Then raise your eyes, and tune your songs;
*   The Saviour lives again!*
Not all the bolts and bars of death
*   The Conqueror could detain:*

High o'er the angelic bands he rears
*   His once dishonoured head;*
And through unnumber'd years he reigns,
*   Who dwelt among the dead.*

  Philip Doddridge (1702–51)

Imitator of Mantegna,
The Resurrection (perhaps 1460–1550)

APPEARANCE TO MARY

The first day of the week cometh Mary Magdalene early, when it was yet dark, unto the sepulchre, and seeth the stone taken away from the sepulchre... Mary stood without at the sepulchre weeping: and as she wept, she stooped down, and looked into the sepulchre, and seeth two angels in white sitting, the one at the head, and the other at the feet, where the body of Jesus had lain. And they say unto her, Woman, why weepest thou? She saith unto them, Because they have taken away my Lord, and I know not where they have laid him. And when she had thus said, she turned herself back, and saw Jesus standing, and knew not that it was Jesus.

Jesus saith unto her, Woman, why weepest thou? whom seekest thou? She, supposing him to be the gardener, saith unto him, Sir, if thou have borne him hence, tell me where thou hast laid him, and I will take him away. Jesus saith unto her, Mary. She turned herself, and saith unto him, Rabboni; which is to say, Master.

Jesus saith unto her, Touch me not; for I am not yet ascended to my Father: but go to my brethren and say unto them, I ascend unto my Father, and your Father; and to my God, and your God.

Mary Magdalene came and told the disciples that she had seen the Lord, and that he had spoken these things unto her.

John 20:1, 11–18

The resurrection of Jesus had a far deeper significance than what happened to the flesh. It meant the resurrection of spirit beyond the needs of any carnal body. Therefore, it was not necessary for the disciples to see the resurrected Jesus, nor for the tomb-keepers to observe him. The Roman soldiers guarded the sepulchre lest his body should be stolen away, but they were not able to testify to his resurrection either. Much less were casual passers-by.

The first person to discover the resurrection of Jesus that morning was Mary Magdalene whose soul had once been possessed with seven devils. The resurrection of Jesus was resurrection for such miserable persons as she, for ruined souls. To those who cannot grasp this meaning, resurrection remains an insoluble enigma, an empty falsehood, a prick of doubt. It is an everlasting secret. Not a few of us seem inclined to deny this miracle. If we are reluctant to accept sinners as friends, it means that we belong to the sceptics who deny the fact of resurrection. Let us, therefore, remember that the first witness who saw the figure of Jesus the morning of his resurrection had been a prostitute.

Toyohiko Kagawa (1888–1960)

Master of the Lehman Crucifixion
(active c. 1352–99),
Noli Me Tangere

THE EMMAUS ROAD

And, behold, two of them went that same day to a village called Emmaus, which was from Jerusalem about threescore furlongs. And they talked together of all these things which had happened. And it came to pass, that, while they communed together and reasoned, Jesus himself drew near, and went with them. But their eyes were holden that they should not know him. And he said unto them, What manner of communications are these that ye have one to another, as ye walk, and are sad? And the one of them, whose name was Cleopas, answering said unto him, Art thou only a stranger in Jerusalem, and hast not known the things which are come to pass there in these days? And he said unto them, What things? And they said unto him, Concerning Jesus of Nazareth, which was a prophet mighty in deed and word before God and all the people: and how the chief priests and our rulers delivered him to be condemned to death, and have crucified him...

Then he said unto them, O fools, and slow of heart to believe all that the prophets have spoken: ought not Christ to have suffered these things, and to enter into his glory? And beginning at Moses and all the prophets, he expounded unto them in all the scriptures the things concerning himself.

Luke 24:13–20, 25–27

Paul Bril (1554–1626),
The Journey to Emmaus

For a person came, and lived and loved, and did and taught, and died and rose again, and lives on by his power and his spirit for ever within us and amongst us, so unspeakably rich and yet so simple, so sublime and yet so homely, so divinely above us precisely in being so divinely near – that his character and teaching require, for an ever fuller yet never complete understanding, the varying study, and different experiments and applications, embodiments and unrollings of all the races and civilizations, of all the individual and corporate, the simultaneous and successive experiences of the human race to the end of time. If there is nothing shifting or fitful or simply changing about him, there are everywhere energy and expansion, thought and emotion, effort and experience, joy and sorrow, loneliness and conflict, interior trial and triumph, exterior defeat and supplantation: particular affections, particular humiliations, homely labour, a homely heroism, greatness throughout in littleness. And in him, for the first and last time, we find an insight so unique, a personality so strong and supreme, as to teach us, once for all, the true attitude towards suffering... With him, and alone with him and those who still learn and live from and by him, there is the union of the clearest, keenest sense of all the mysterious depth and breadth and length and height of human sadness, suffering, and sin, *and*, in spite of this and through this and at the end of this, a note of conquest and of triumphant joy.

Friedrich von Hügel (1852–1925)

SUPPER AT EMMAUS

And they drew nigh unto the village, whither they went: and he made as though he would have gone further. But they constrained him, saying, Abide with us: for it is toward evening, and the day is far spent. And he went in to tarry with them. And it came to pass, as he sat at meat with them, he took bread, and blessed it, and brake, and gave to them. And their eyes were opened, and they knew him; and he vanished out of their sight. And they said one to another, Did not our heart burn within us, while he talked with us by the way, and while he opened to us the scriptures?

And they rose up the same hour, and returned to Jerusalem, and found the eleven gathered together, and them that were with them, saying, The Lord is risen indeed, and hath appeared to Simon. And they told what things were done in the way, and how he was known of them in breaking of bread.

Luke 24:28–35

The friends of Jesus saw him and heard him only a few times after that Easter morning, but their lives were completely changed. What seemed to be the end proved to be the beginning; what seemed to be a cause for fear proved to be a cause for courage; what seemed to be defeat proved to be victory; and what seemed to be the basis for despair proved to be the basis for hope. Suddenly a wall becomes a gate, and although we are not able to say with much clarity or precision what lies beyond that gate, the tone of all that we do and say on our way to the gate changes drastically.

Henri J.M. Nouwen (1932–97)

Michelangelo Merisi da Caravaggio
(1571–1610), *The Supper at Emmaus*

DOUBTING THOMAS

Then the same day at evening, being the first day of the week, when the doors were shut where the disciples were assembled for fear of the Jews, came Jesus and stood in the midst, and saith unto them, Peace be unto you. And when he had so said, he shewed unto them his hands, and his side. Then were the disciples glad, when they saw the Lord...

But Thomas, one of the twelve, called Didymus, was not with them when Jesus came. The other disciples therefore said unto him, We have seen the Lord. But he said unto them, Except I shall see in his hands the print of the nails, and put my finger into the print of the nails, and thrust my hand into his side, I will not believe.

And after eight days again his disciples were within, and Thomas with them: then came Jesus, the doors being shut, and stood in the midst, and said, Peace be unto you. Then saith he to Thomas, Reach hither thy finger, and behold my hands; and reach hither thy hand, and thrust it into my side: and be not faithless, but believing. And Thomas answered and said unto him, My Lord and my God. Jesus saith unto him, Thomas, because thou hast seen me, thou hast believed: blessed are they that have not seen, and yet have believed.

John 20:19–20, 24–29

JESUS OF THE SCARS

If we have never sought, we seek thee now;
Thine eyes burn through the dark, our only stars;
We must have sight of thorn-pricks on thy brow,
We must have thee, O Jesus of the Scars.

The heavens frighten us; they are too calm;
In all the universe we have no place.
Our wounds are hurting us; where is thy balm?
Lord Jesus, by thy scars we claim thy grace.

If when the doors are shut, thou drawest near,
Only reveal those hands, that side of thine;
We know today what wounds are, have no fear,
Show us thy scars, we know the countersign.

The other gods were strong; but thou wast weak:
They rode, but thou didst stumble to a throne;
But to our wounds God's wounds alone can speak,
And not a god has wounds, but thou alone.

Edward Shillito (1872–1948)

Bernardo Strozzi (1581–1644),
Doubting Thomas

ASCENSION

Then the eleven disciples went away into Galilee, into a mountain where Jesus had appointed them. And when they saw him, they worshipped him: but some doubted. And Jesus came and spake unto them, saying, All power is given unto me in heaven and in earth.

Matthew 28:16–18

When they therefore were come together, they asked of him, saying, Lord, wilt thou at this time restore again the kingdom to Israel? And he said unto them, It is not for you to know the times or the seasons, which the Father hath put in his own power. But ye shall receive power, after that the Holy Ghost is come upon you: and ye shall be witnesses unto me both in Jerusalem, and in all Judea, and in Samaria, and unto the uttermost part of the earth. And when he had spoken these things, while they beheld, he was taken up; and a cloud received him out of their sight.

Acts 1:6–9

Jesus does not return to his Father in isolation. It was the incorporeal *logos* that descended among men. But today it is the Word made flesh, at the same time true God and true man, that enters the Kingdom of heaven. Jesus takes there with him the human nature in which he is clothed. He opens the gates of the Kingdom to humanity. We take possession, in some way by anticipation, of the blessings which are offered to us and possible for us. Places are reserved for us in the Kingdom provided we continue faithful. Our presence is desired and awaited there.

So the ascension renders the thought of heaven more present and more alive for us. Do we think enough of our permanent dwelling-place? For most Christians heaven is envisaged as a kind of postscript, an appendix to a book of which life on earth constitutes the actual text. But the contrary is true. Our earthly life is merely the preface to the book. Life in heaven will be the text – a text without end.

A monk of the Eastern church

Attributed to Jacopo di Cione and workshop,
The Ascension (1370–71)

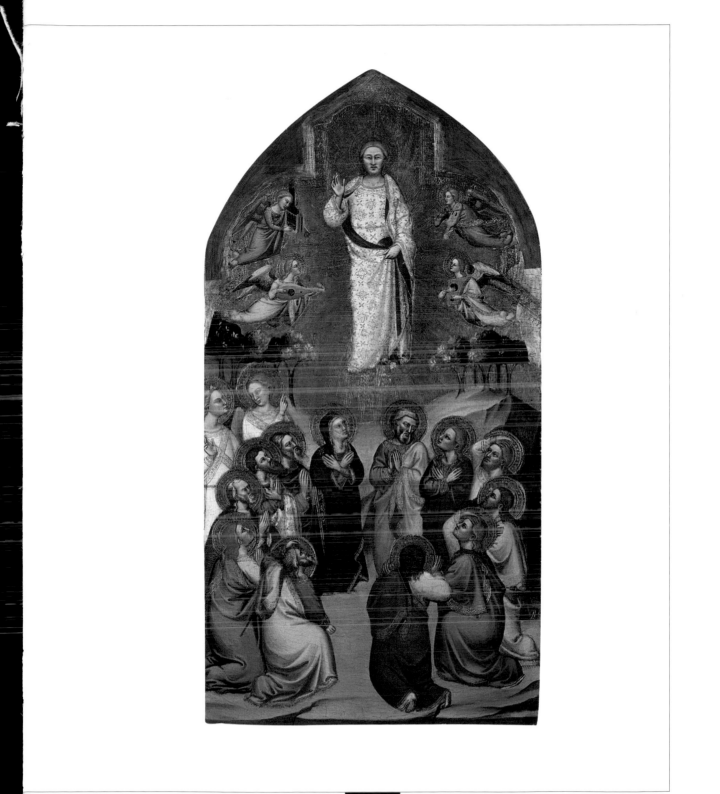

SAVIOUR

For God so loved the world, that he gave his only begotten Son, that whosoever believeth in him should not perish, but have everlasting life. For God sent not his Son into the world to condemn the world; but that the world through him might be saved.

John 3:16–17

Andrea Previtali (active 1502; d. 1528),
Salvator Mundi